MILLIONS AND MILLIONS OF CRYSTALS

MILLIONS AND MILLIONS OF CRYSTALS

By Roma Gans

Illustrated by Giulio Maestro

THOMAS Y. CROWELL COMPANY · NEW YORK

LET'S·READ·AND·FIND·OUT SCIENCE BOOKS

Editors: *DR. ROMA GANS,* Professor Emeritus of Childhood Education, Teachers College, Columbia University

DR. FRANKLYN M. BRANLEY, Chairman and Astronomer of The American Museum– Hayden Planetarium

*AVAILABLE IN SPANISH

Library of Congress Cataloging in Publication Data
Gans, Roma/Millions and millions of crystals.
SUMMARY: Describes the characteristics, formation, and uses of various types of crystals.
1. Crystallography—Juvenile literature. [1. Crystals] I. Maestro, Giulio, illus. II. Title.
QD906.3.G36 548 72-7547   ISBN 0-690-54029-9 ISBN 0-690-54030-2 (lib. bdg.)

1   2   3   4   5   6   7   8   9   10

MILLIONS AND MILLIONS OF CRYSTALS

LET'S
READ
AND
FIND
OUT

There are millions and millions of crystals in the world.

You have walked on them.

You have kicked them and tossed them.

You have even eaten crystals.

When you eat the sugar on your cereal, you are eating crystals of sugar.

When you eat salt on your hamburger, you are eating crystals of salt.

Sugar and salt crystals are bright and sparkling.
Put a few crystals of salt or sugar on a piece of dark
   cloth or paper.
Hold it in the sunlight.
Now look at the crystals through a magnifying glass.
You will see that the crystals have flat shiny sides.

The sand you play in has thousands of tiny rock crystals in it.

Large rocks may have crystals of minerals in them.

Some may be pink; some, white or blue or other colors.

Many are too small for you to see.

Have you ever walked on fresh snow?
Then you have walked on the most beautiful crystals
of all.

While snow is falling, you can see separate flakes on
your coat sleeve.
Each one is like a sparkling star.

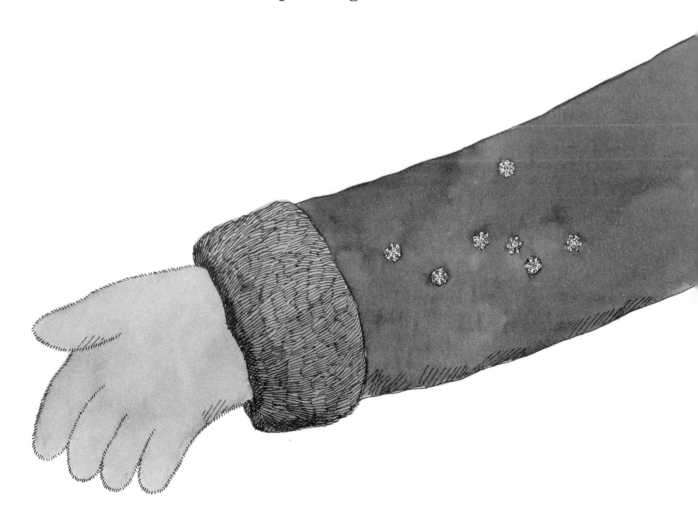

Each separate snowflake is a crystal.
You wish they would never melt so you could collect
them.

Some kinds of crystals are set in rings and pins.
Diamonds, rubies, and garnets are crystals.
When they are dug from the ground, they do not look
like jewels.

They sparkle after they have been cut and polished.

Crystals are made of atoms.

An atom is too small for you to see even with a microscope.

A grain of salt is a crystal. But even such a tiny crystal is made of millions of atoms.

The atoms of salt collect together.

They do not come together any old way.

The atoms fit together in a special way.

Then more and more atoms fasten onto the first few atoms.

As they fasten together, the atoms grow into a salt crystal.

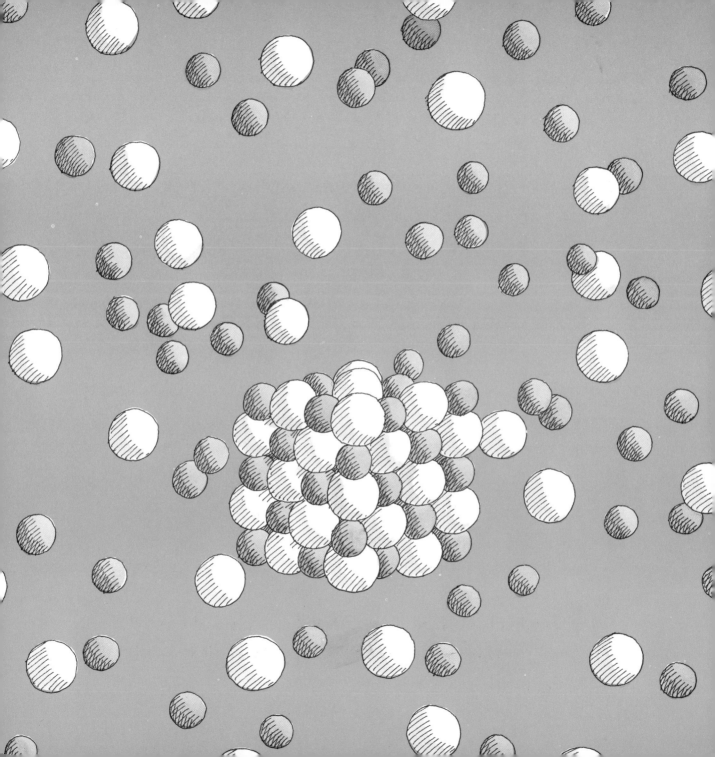

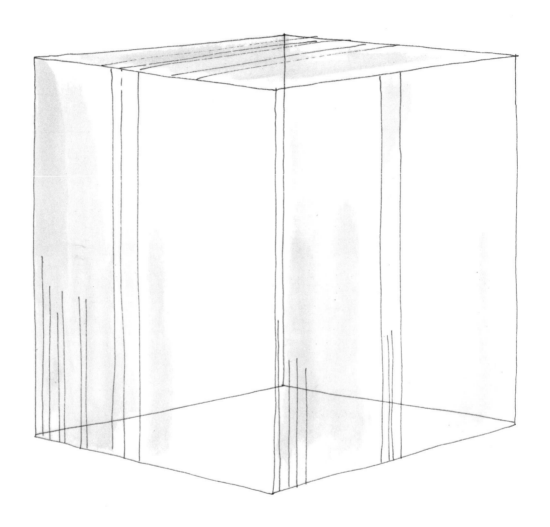

The salt crystal is box-shaped. Each side of the
"box" is the same size and shape. We call it a cube.
This crystal has six sides.

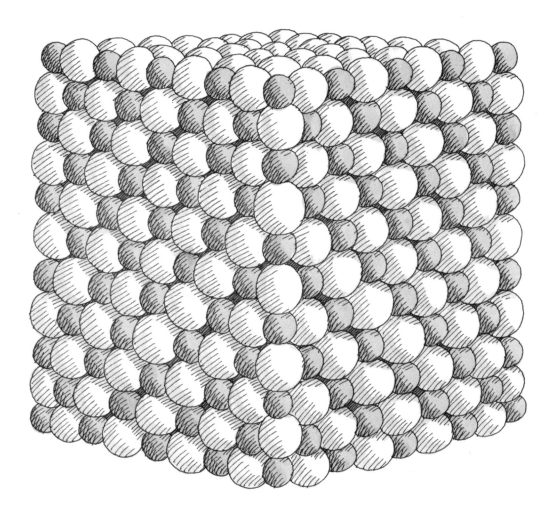

The atoms that make salt always come together in the same way.

Atoms join together in a different way to make a
  diamond crystal.

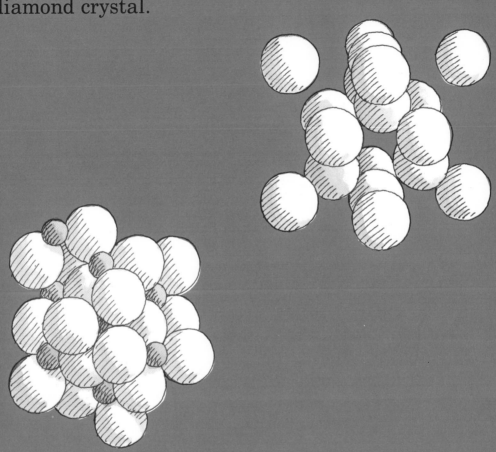

And a ruby crystal is different from a diamond
  crystal.
Each kind of crystal is made by atoms in its own
  special way.

In mica crystals atoms come together in thin, flat layers. You can see mica crystals shining in stones and pebbles.

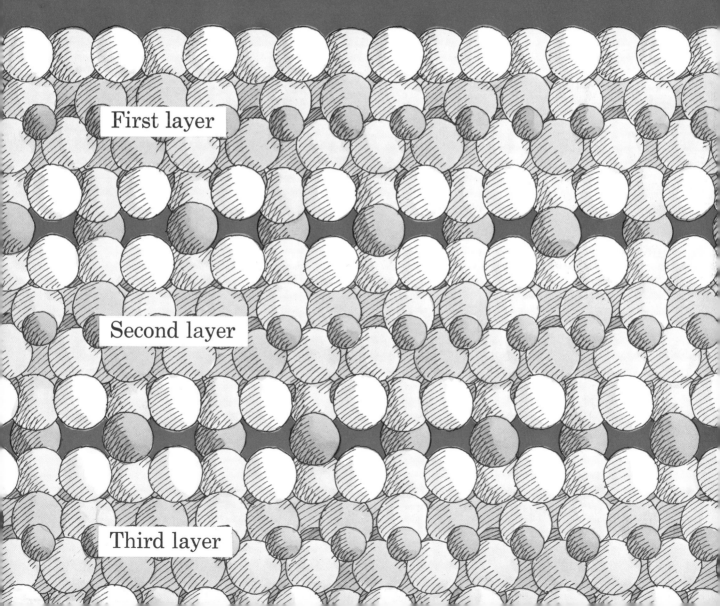

First layer

Second layer

Third layer

Mica cracks along its thin layers. You can peel off
layer after layer by lifting each layer with a pin.

Some crystals are made so they crack in different ways. Garnets crack along slanted lines.

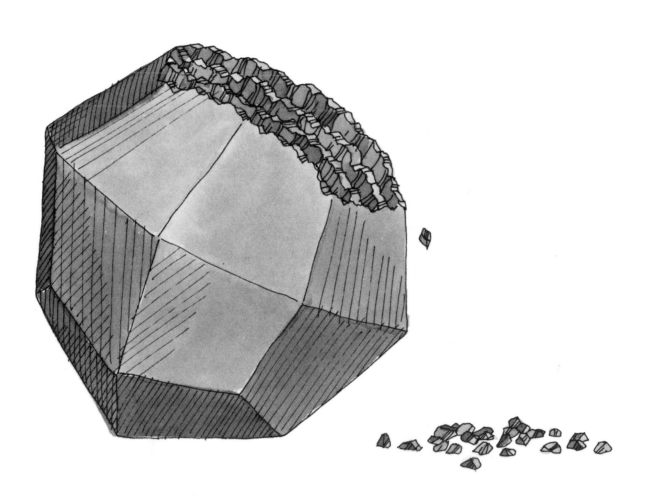

Some crystals surprise us.

Metals, like iron and copper, do not look to us like crystals.

But their atoms come together in neat patterns that can be seen by looking through a very strong microscope.

So we know they are crystals.

Glass sparkles like diamonds and other crystals.

But the atoms in glass are not arranged in a pattern, the way crystals are.

So glass is *not* a crystal.

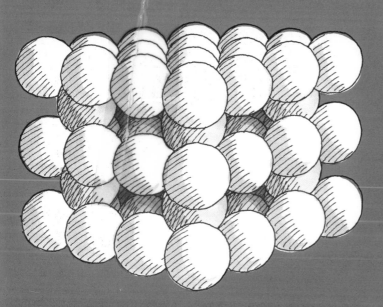

Iron atoms

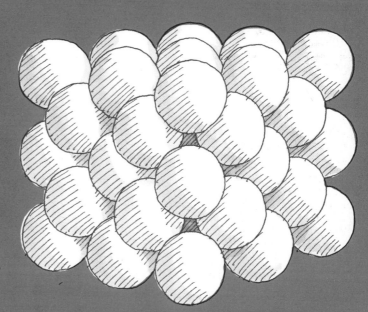

Copper atoms

21

Each crystal needs room to grow.
If a growing crystal is crowded, it cannot become a
  perfect crystal.
A perfect salt crystal is a perfect cube.
The cube may be squeezed and become lopsided.
When it gets crowded by other salt crystals, it does
  not grow six perfect sides.
Then it is not a perfect cube. But it is still a crystal.
Few crystals of any kind are perfect.

Nearly perfect rock crystals are found in caves.
There is plenty of room for them to grow
    there.
Some grow down from the top of the cave.

Some grow up from the floor of the cave.
They grow slowly.
The atoms come together and make beautiful large
  crystals.

Crystals are also found in geodes.

A geode is a bubble that was made in the earth's rocky crust.

When the crust slowly cooled, the round bubble was formed.

The outside of the bubble became hard rock.

The inside of the bubble cooled slowly, and crystals were made. The crystals line the hollow inside.

When a geode is split open, you can see the crystals.

Some are lavender or black or gray.

Some are clear and sparkling.

The next time you are out walking, look for a stone
   that has different colors showing.
Wet it so that you can see the separate colors better.
You may see small white, pink, and black parts in
   the stone.

These are crystals that were made millions of years
ago while the stone was hot and melted.
If the stone cooled slowly, many atoms could join
together, and big crystals could form in the stone.
If the stone cooled fast, not so many atoms could
come together before it hardened.
Then the crystals would be smaller.

You can find different kinds of crystals in sand and
    gravel.
They may be pink, white, black, or other colors.
They may be broken parts of big crystals.
Some may be shiny like bright jewels.

Many people collect crystals.

You can collect them too.

You can find out more about them.

Then you will become a crystal expert —
a crystallographer!

ABOUT THE AUTHOR

Roma Gans has called children "enlightened, excited citizens." She believes in the fundamental theory that children are eager to learn and will whet their own intellectual curiosity if they have stimulating teachers and books. She herself is the author of eight books in the Let's-Read-and-Find-Out series.

Dr. Gans received her B.S. from Columbia Teachers College and her Ph.D. from Columbia University. She began her work in the educational field in the public schools of the Middle West as a teacher, supervisor, and assistant superintendent of schools. She is Professor Emeritus of Childhood Education at Teachers College, Columbia University, and lectures extensively throughout this country and Canada.

Dr. Gans lives in West Redding, Connecticut, where she enjoys observing the many aspects of nature.

ABOUT THE ILLUSTRATOR

Giulio Maestro was born in New York City and studied painting and print-making at the Cooper Union Art School and at Pratt Graphics Center. He has illustrated many books for young readers, and is also well known for his beautiful hand lettering and book-jacket design. *The Tortoise's Tug of War*, which he both wrote and illustrated, was chosen by the American Institute of Graphic Arts as one of the best children's books of the year.

Mr. Maestro lives in New Haven, Connecticut.